THE LONG AND THE SHORT OF IT

Other poetry by the same author:

About Nottingham, Byron Press, 1971
Egils Saga: Versions of the Poems, Dent Everyman,
1975, reprinted as an Everyman Classic, 1984 and 1993
Studying Grosz on the Bus, Peterloo Poets, 1989
Flying to Romania, Sows Ear Press, 1992
One for the Piano, Redbeck Press, 1997
On the Track, Redbeck Press, 2000
A World Perhaps: New & Selected Poems,
Trent Editions and Sows Ear Press, 2002

THE LONG
AND
THE SHORT OF IT

⌀

JOHN LUCAS

RED
BECK
PRESS

2004

The Long and the Short of It
is published by Redbeck Press,
24 Aireville Road, Frizinghall,
Bradford BD9 4HH

Design and Print by Tony Ward,
Arc & Throstle Press, Hanholme Mill,
Todmorden, Lancs., OL14 6DA

ISBN 1-904338-22-4

Redbeck Press acknowledges financial assistance
from the Arts Council England – Yorkshire.

ACKNOWLEDGEMENTS:

Some of these poems first appeared in the follow-
ing periodicals: *The Coffee House, Critical Sur-
vey, the Dark Horse, The Frogmore Papers, Other
Poetry, The Penniless Press, Poetry Wales.*

"Lament for a Dead Son" is a revised version of
the poem-translation that first appeared in *Egils
Saga: Versions of the Poems,* Dent Everyman.

Thanks are due to NTU for its generous support.
Cover design from a painting "Ben and Catherine
in Chagford Churchyard" by Pauline Lucas.

for Hugh Underhill and Peter Widdowson

Not for victory
but for the day's work done
as well as I was able

Charles Reznikoff

CONTENTS

III

I

GOOD FOR YOU

Bedbound, sipping tinily at air,
you had, it seemed, gone beyond words,
and, in your phrase for small ones
tired at the end of a long, packed day,
were "utterly lost to the world."

But when I eased that cork up
and out, its brief sigh woke
something behind your sightless eyes.

"Just pouring myself a drink, Mum."
                                        "Good
for you." Habitual solicitude
and, I think, that old gaiety
astir once more in your repeat
whisper "Good for you."

11

OTHER HOUSES, OTHER LIVES

i.m. my mother, Phyllis Joan Lucas, 1910-2003

I

Driving, I think each place I speed through means
tales that you chose to linger in like years.
Holne, for one, where Gertie, high on the moors,
aghast as Heinkels wheeled away from Exeter,
"dropped like a stone" from off her postman horse.

For weeks she plucked out gorse spines from her flesh,
even at church, where she and Florrie sang
"almost in tune", while in the next-door Arms
Fred lasted out his pint, then, service done,
marched with Florrie back to Wellpritton Farm.

"At Spitchwick, that was. In its village hall
they'd met and courted at the weekly dance,
the fiddler whistling all he couldn't bow,
And Fred's round face so lit up you could read by it
when she said 'yes' those seventy years ago."

And here's *Two Bridges*, tearooms shut and barred
as that hot day you trudged here with a young
grandson (now a father); nothing to do but turn
and struggle back to Chagford. "But that night
we slept the sleep of the just, I'll have you learn."

From you I learnt, too, much of village scandal:
the grocer who kept three wives "round and about",
the Dame who huffed "'we never back up in Devon' –
because she couldn't!"; the sexton who downed ale
"as though he thought he'd find none up in heaven,

and cut the grass no better than he shaved";
the wife that left him for "a fancy Dan,"
who, "so she *claimed*", then vanished with her purse
while she worked bar-hours. "But she chitters still
with twill-cord tourists, gives them chapter and verse

of tattle in exchange for port." A laugh,
a wry shake of the head, then "have I *told* you …."
Grieved by cruelty, you found delight
in waywardness and wouldn't censure lives
"by no means *comme-il-faut*" – a phrase you liked

to harry prudes with and the hunting set.
But laughter thinned as friends and cousins died.
and though I saw you turn impatiently
from the *obits.*, that couldn't stop the death
you dreaded most. You wrote, "The end for me."

But not before more weddings starred more years,
more great-grandchildren, then your ninetieth birthday,
and village pantos where from the front row
your stage whisper – "Idle Jack's no cherub,
and the Cook! My Giddy Aunt!" – quite stole the show.

Arthritis slowed your body, though, and from
the house that looked towards Meldon, where you'd both
"come rain, come shine", made tracks through fern and broom,
arm-in-arm, companionable, content,
alone now, you moved to a rented room.

Then, heavy, stiff-limbed, to another town.
"Only six miles away but it might be
the other side of the moon for all I care;
like this I'm no more use to anyone."
So: a short, last illness, and you were gone.

13

II

Oxford in Wartime. Nash's premonitory oil
views Hopkins's "towery city" from a hill
up which lumber numerous tanks, massed steel
to keep at bay the White Roses of Death
that Hitler's planes would scatter and let fall
on the Heart of England, poisoning its sweet breath
of Culture (did Nash fear?).

                            My own lack-culture
father drove tanks. Suppose that he could steer
to where I'm standing now, the dreaming spires
over his head at first then falling back
while up from '43 to Liverpool's Tate
he comes to join me at this century's start,
as if no more than years kept us apart?

No more? But more than enough! When he came back
I was the one to whom he couldn't talk.

And so these endless dreams of corridors
whose doors all open onto other doors
through which are doors that lead to corridors,
And yet however far I'm made to walk
past or through doors, the man I'm looking for
evades me, and there's no room to sit and talk.

Yet that most recent dream. I'm in a room
where you, as ever immaculately dressed,
collar and tie, coat buttoned, scant hair combed,
sit straight-backed at a table, suitcase locked.
Although you're six years dead, you've come to call.
Then why do I feel apprehensive gloom
seeing Mum beside you? Ah, this isn't a room,
I suddenly know, this is a Transit Hall.

I start to speak, then see you tug her sleeve.
You don't hear what I say. You have to leave.

14

III

Why *can't* we live in years as in a house,
throw open doors, know ourselves free to roam
from room to room, say "this is as it was,
this chair and Morrison table show the same
each time it's summer, '42,
                              and now
Christmas '70 waits in the next room."

Look! Here's my mother bent to darn a sock,
blackout curtains drawn tight, while *her* mother
knits soldier scarves or reaches for a pack
of Weights, exhales and watches thin smoke dither
around that light flex where a thick
crust of glued flies hangs.
                              Now see it waver

as the door opens. A small boy steps inside,
followed by his sister. Clutching rag books,
they press against their mother who will read
them bedtime tales.
                      But now, older, she takes
grandchildren on her lap, and when her head
bends to the words, her hair no longer sparks

with coppery glints, and looking round I see
a different room.
                    She listens. In the hall
her husband props his golf bag, calls to say
he'll cook their dinner.
                          He is not yet ill,
and her pretended, small, impatient sigh
turns to candid laughter.

                    I want this spell
of happiness to last but know it can't.

The room is emptied, first of him, then her.

Now see a family gather among graves.
"United in love" is carved into the stone
we gaze at.
                    Will it last out Chagford weather?
For some years yet, no doubt, and while that's scant
solace once years that housed their lives are gone,
lives that they made, and, making, blessed, go on,
and with them other houses, other lives.

BROKEN CONNECTION

It's Sunday, six o'clock. I lift the phone
to make the usual call, then put it down.
Though your "Hello", Mum, echoes in my head,
I can't talk (can I?) to someone three months dead.

12.10.'03

PAINTING THE KITCHEN RED

That swanky swerve, sweep, slap and flick
of his six-inch brush at each bare surface, deft
reach into corners where dust thought itself safe,
and hour-by-hour skirting board, lintel and shelf
turn carmine bright. What's new glistens

like ripe, beaded flesh against chipped
lino, the gas-stove's flaked enamel, windows
up to let Easter's breeze dispel
distemper's piss-smell; and all day
tea, iced biscuits and cakes

that rose the previous evening
warm from their tray are guided
into his mouth teased open
by her suddenly candid fingers,
spicy with spring's unique, cinnamon promise.

AIMS AND OBJECTS: A MISSION STATEMENT

Today a pew end thumped my wife,
yesterday a swinging shutter
cuffed her, and once last week
thwack went her knee against a table leg
as she leant to freshen a bowl
of garden flowers. I have noticed other women
tend to collisions with objects
we men avoid. Thus certain experts
(archimandrites of our secular age)
tell us that women lack Spatial
Awareness. I disagree.

At home, or out and about, straining
to peer at rood screens
or craving a distant view,
women assume trust is a blessing
that will not let them down. Men,
fearing the worst, centre their aim
on what they hope to control: dogs,
dress code, bladders. Stockades
of iron, outgunned, will! It could be
dignity at bay from premature
baldness, or muffing a catch,
or the corduroy expert unsure who said
"I dare do all that may become a man."

Settle for less than all. Accept
each day to be rebuked by mute insistence,
whether this prove an unbiddable
zip, some ball or dog that will
not come to hand, or, now I think of it,

a woman who, rubbing her bruised hip-bone,
watches in silent joy as angels
tumble through clouds,
their hands raised in greeting.

ON FAROS BEACH

for Ben and Catherine

I

Six o'clock sun and headlines
pestered by breeze. From our narrow beach
I watch boats steer to local fishing grounds

or, more riskily, head for gulfs
where summer storms can smash unwary vessels.
That couldn't happen here,

surely, in this land-locked reach of sea,
the worst of it, as now, no more than
lambs' wool snagged on wavelets?

And thinking this, I'm suddenly
back to sheep wandering at ease
fields beyond an old house deep

in pastoral Sussex. There,
seven years since,
July sun blest your wedding.

II

So many folk had come together then:
families, friends, some from America,
Catherine's parents all the way from Oz,

and mine, who'd driven from their Devon home
and who, another gran cheery beside them,
laugh from the afternoon's green holm:

permanent rejoicing (though all
three are sunk in earth now.)
And then, next day, we strolled

along a hedged-in lane (to where, at Bateman's',
hopes guttered like headland fires
as Ypres's mud closed over an only son.)

III

A wedding's chance had brought us to that spot,
as years ago chance dropped me on this island
across from whose calm waters I would learn

Mycenae's hill glooms. Agamemnon,
Clytemnestra, Iphigenia, Elektra – Atreus' House
wrecked for all time by the sacrifice of love.

So, in 1915, Henry James feared the going
of those "long safe centuries" he
figured in the "spread of the great trees,

the mere gathers in the bluey-white
curtains of cottage windows, the curl
of tinted smoke from old chimneys" – like those

at Haremere Hall and Bateman's. "More
substance in our enmities than in our love" – Yeats'
lament for bodies sprawled in country lanes,

and in 1938 a voice wryly proclaimed
"Force alas is the ultimate reality,"
a wind to scatter hope like paper scraps

that fall as dragons' teeth and sow
desolation's crop, its poppy growth
bloodying each town on ruin's map.

IV

Unlooked-for wind now on Faros' beach
bellies the paper's auguries of war,
spray on my glasses turns the sky

craquelure, the evening sun is doused,
and water darkens at a sudden chill.
Time to go, and time to recollect

again those places waiting to welcome us,
paysages moralisées of clement freshness,
where sheep wander, symbol, it's true, of sacrifice

(like these white forms that shatter in the wind),
but places, too, where "grass eternal
springs", persistent, nourishing

and actual, like love's durative green.

                                        Aegina, September, 2003

Faros is the Greek for lighthouse;
"A voice wryly proclaimed." E.M. Forster, who in the autumn of 1938 gave a BBC talk
called "Two Cheers for Democracy", later retitled "What I Believe"; "clement fresh-
ness". When St Clement went into exile with his converts in the 2nd century AD, "their
sufferings were intense due to the lack of fresh water. Clement struck the ground with a
pick axe, and immediately a stream of water gushed forth. Enraged at this miracle, his
persecutors tied an anchor about his neck and hurled him into the sea. Upon the prayers
of his followers, however, the waters drew back, revealing a small temple where the body
of the saint was found." George Ferguson, Signs & Symbols *in Christian Art*, OUP, 1954.
"And still the grass eternal springs." John Clare, *The Flitting*

WEDDING SONG

For Emma and Chris

Adieu this day to last week's cold and rain:
There's sun enough to coax folk out of doors
As clouds dwindle over the stone-capped moors,
Their upland sheep and fields of shimmering grain.
      And so, clear of the Main
Street's well-suited pseuds, thrasonical boors,
And all their brassy tones that ding the ears
With news of deals gone B-Side, of turf wars
Between old friends (ending – how else? – in tears)
      I walked abroad to a cheer
Of blackbirds' song at Ashford-in-the Water
Beside the Wye, a place to drown sour thoughts
A while at least, musing on Spenser's rhyme,
How it might serve to celebrate my daughter
      For whom, this summertime
      I wanted words to chime
With her wedding day, that comes in high July.
      Run softly till I end my song, sweet Wye!

And first I thought how, forty years ago,
I met a girl from Derbyshire's bare hills.
Sheep-skulls, frail as parchment, littered the mill-
Stone crags and peaks, she told me, while below,
      Where limestone rivers flow
Through blue-john caves, each coalmine's squealing wheel
Brought men to light who'd scrum through a wire gate
To pass round jokes and fags, then, down-on-heel,
Beside a favoured inn door squat to wait
      The landlord's pleasure. Her spate

Of words washed bright a memory of Edale,
A schoolboy's Easter jaunt, a frost-clean trail
Down to the Noe past rams at bay, their horns
Fabulous as the otter sleeking its tail
  In a world that seemed newborn
  As now, all ills forsworn
For a wedding day that comes in high July.
  Run softly till I end my song, sweet Wye!

Years later, married now, that girl and I
With our young son arrived in Nottingham
In soot-clogged autumn heat which soon became
Swept out by arctic winds, when each night sky
  Glittered with stars pinned high
Over stunned white streets. We thought a new Ice Age
Had come, and fogs, that swaddled the town in gloom
Of sulphur fumes, seemed its assured presage,
Pronunciamento of a come-soon doom.
  Instead to our front room
One evening that December, new life came
Gusting in, and its fierce leap of flame
Loosened the cold's hard grip, so we might be
Warmed by a daughter as by son, untamed
  Spirits who ran clear and free
  To bring a family
At length to this wedding day in high July.
  Run softly till I end my song, sweet Wye!

And now my song comes to its solving close
As family and friends approach a place
Linked by its stream to other sites of grace,
(As Wye to Derwent to Noe) as history flows
  Through many caves and hollows
Down to one source, as rivers further apart –
The Don, the Dart – join "where all waters meet",
That wellspring Wordsworth called "the human heart"

Common to northern hill as southern street,
    A rill of words to greet
All wedding guests on this bright summer's day,
Old and new friends and family: they say
"Well met at Ashford, whether it's from North
Or other compass points you've found your way,
    This spot of Derbyshire earth
    Is now of special worth
As Chris and Emma's bridal place." And my song
    Is ended, though love, like the Wye, runs on.

July, 1999

25

TWO POEMS FOR A GRANDDAUGHTER

Amanda Kelly Caitlin Riney-Lucas, born 6.8.'04

i) A Launching

If history, as the Australian poet claims,
Means the voyages of families down their names,
Then those heavy-cargoed tales of Blue Ribbon rancour,
Of Queens and Men of War, must heave to and all drop anchor,
While out from port, as though taking a dander
To see the new world, comes this yare barque named
For Love's conjugation:
                              Amo, Amas, Amat, Amanda

ii) Six Months Out

Alone on the white stretch
of your unruckled mat, you
oh, so slowly founder, then turn
turtle at some unfathomable tide.

Nothing so confident as your blue gaze,
your – can it be? – knowledge that rescue
is, as always, to hand,

that yet again this reach
of arms, setting you right,
will guide you surely to where,

past your horizon's Now,
days like sea-lanes
widen into years

II

THE MEETING ON ACHARNON STREET

for George Dandoulakis

Into that teeming street plugged
to the city's heart I watched you
bustle from out the narrow lane where pain

for so long crowded our lives,
gutters I trawled for coins
to buy our daily bread, where mother's

other children ran away in blood,
and rumours of work hung thin as smoke
above the kafeneon's *tavli* tables.

Years that stumbled, their arms full of loss.

But now your step was eager, purposive,
so that my own pace quickened,
needing to keep your back in view. "Father?"

In that unhindered light you turned.
Younger than when I saw you last, your eyes
welcomed my unasked question. "I am

very happy now, my son" you said, your
stubbled, carefree smile bright-
ening, getting sweeter

as if you could not possibly be dead.

TOWN AND COUNTRY

"Yeero, yeero," the Greeks shrug, "round and around",
and I think, *polis kai kora, rus et urbs;*
one day you're snuffing up basil and camomile,
the next you're down to lungsful of city fug.

So, here on a rustic balcony, Aegina's sun
heats jasmine's honey and only the flick of a swift
disturbs my green, solitary thoughts; yet I'm a mile
(at most) from the port town's fishy stinks, its hullabaloo.

Well, better *tzitzikis* sifting through gravel all day
than a hornet swarm of mopeds and those chug-a-chug
liquorice earmuffs. *"Malakas* to that", I say
– but know the mood won't last. Come nightfall I'll hanker

for the wine and spicy talk of a thronged taverna;
much as a Nottingham elbows-in pizzeria
beats rose-red mansions half as old as time
where waiters bend among cultivated whispers. And though

Cotswold Ways may start from the Mile End Road,
I doubt I'd make the trip. Don't look for me under your
green wellies, I mean, I'm like Manoli who swore
he'd be an atheist if God allowed.

I'd leave the town but the town won't let me go,
not far at least, nor for long. *Yeero, yeero.*

Manoli: a character in Nick Papandreou's novel, *Father Dancing.*

READING OVID IN BEESTON

Geranium red is not the red of blood,
so how come that as each new petal fell
and splashed the grass, it could have been a sigh
like breeze-filled branches I heard well
up from the ground beneath this flawless sky.

Drowsing, I thought, the bird that dropped the seed,
translated from Africa to England's May,
had lifted it from an Aegean island
where, scythed and spread to sun, the dead plant lay
as though prepared for some ambiguous garland.

Trying to rewind change can do no good,
but now I spooled from petal back to a girl
emerging from Saronic blue, then, seized
in a taloned grip, limbs flailing, and the swirl
of waters as she's plunged to deepest grief.

Later, thrown clear, she's buried in a wood
by herdsmen, desperate to hide
the guilt of gods who killed because they could.
And then the flowers come up from her grave,
geraniums, red as guilt, and spread worldwide.

FOUR REPORTS FROM THE FRONT

1) Peace Work

for Derrick Buttress

The broom is in the cupboard,
     fresh-starched linen fills the chest,
and bedposts flower with mobcaps
     as maids lie down to rest.

Soon they will rise once more
     to heat the evening tub
for flannelled youths who saunter in
     to quail and syllabub.

"For now and always" Abigail sighs
     "this is my life's routine",
turning the calendar's new leaf
     to August, 1914.

2) The War Effort in Cairo, 1939-45

It is not bugles I hear but a hunting horn. Keith Douglas

Andrew Hughes-Onslow,
Eddy Gathorne-Hardy,
Sholto Douglas,
Lord Dunsany,

Mitzie Duhring,
Birkham Sweet-Escott,
Laurence Grafftey-Smith,
"Momo" Marriot,

"Bolo" Keble,
Pamela Hore-Ruthven,
Sir Noel Beresford-Peirse,
Hugh Seton-Watson,

Lady Keown-Boyd,
Mark Chapman Walker,
"At the Going Down of the Sun"
Etcetera, Etcetera.

(The names are taken from CAIRO IN THE WAR, *1939-45, by Artemis Cooper.)*

3) **Comic Relief**

Knock, Knock. Who's There? The Porter – whose
wormy jokes, the theory is,
produce some easement, then it's back
to supping full of horror stories.

Tonight's News hands us on a plate
charred Lives and Towns – the Fare of War –
then breaks for Satire's Masterpiece:
Bush. Blair. Rumsfeld. Straw.

April, 2003

4) **Bird's Eye View**

This questing cat's imperative
is "To live and not let live."

And look! Here struts Sir Bare-Balls Dog,
Each public way his private bog.

Good people, have you lost your wits?
If not, why favour Thugs and Shits!

PROSPECTS

i.m. Paul O'Flinn

"No-one would sing the virtues of *my* place.
'On 26 Home Close': not quite the ring
of 'Upon Appleton House: To My Lord Fairfax'".
I hear your voice, Paul, see that quick-fade grin:
"not enough class, alas" – those flattened ayes
your minor public school could not erase.

"And Mr. Knightley's prospect, so natural
you'd never think it *built*, unlike the street
we tramp each day in answer to the call
of duty-harassed lives. Not here, the sweet-
especial scene, though we can pay to view
houses and land stolen from us, it's true.

True as Tressell's talk of the Money Trick.
His prospect was of work until you drop,
or being sacked by that boss-addled, sick
gaffer, so Gabriel Varden-like he'd shop
his mates for going slow. 'Get the job through
bodge pronto: no two coats where one will do.'

'Thou'art built with no man's ruine, no man's groane.'
Pull the other! Or call it an ideal
once bearable but now like rubbled stone
dropped in the well of History where 'Unreal'
echoes out of the empty dark. Seal down
the lid and catch a bus back into town."

I try to snare your swift words as they fly
from memory of that cold March London day,
kindle once more your sparky scorn for high-
table talk of "Prospect", and, Paul, I'd lay
good odds that long before our Conference end
your wit, cutting us new vistas, old friend,

34

meant all could join that view leading to where
citizens gather in a public way,
where "Two cross scythes gleam above the rich hair
of people dressed as though for holiday
or 'like a bed of tulips in the sun,'"
where private dream's transmuted into vision,

"our place become the earthly paradise"
William Morris dreamt of for John Ball
(though fouled-up London made him turn his eyes
to Oxfordshire, each tithe barn there, mead hall
and cottage, proof that ideal circumstance
linked work and dwelling in the social dance).

"We'll get there yet" we swore that day in town.
And then, just four days later, you were dead,
your good red heart at last letting you down
after long years singing for daily bread –
for to know "pleasure in the work itself"
made teaching both a means and end of wealth,

so you avowed, knowing how much I loved
Topsy's edict, as you did. Now the breath's
knocked out of us, those many who approved
the prospect that you worked for and bequeath:
a singing school for all alike to share:
a common place, here, now, there, *anywhere.*

August, 2001

BEYOND THE HEADLINES

in memory of Wilfred Page, 1913-1991, and for Arnold Rattenbury

Ex-comrade S., "King Sensitive the First",
CONFESSES RED YEARS TO HAVE BEEN MISTAKE.
Shock-horror news, though nowhere near the worst.
FORMER COMMIE WAS ALWAYS ON THE MAKE,
SOVIET LOVER'S THREAT TO THE FREE WEST,
Or MOLE TOLD KGB OF H BOMB TEST.

No headlines for *this* Death Note. "Wilfred Page
agricultural labourer, Norfolk born."
Aged ten, the boy learnt from his teacher's rage
"Thou shall not muzzle the ox that treads the corn",
a voice raised high for farm workers who'd struck
against the muzzle's choking grip, their luck

Down and out like Wilf's grandfather, too old,
too slow at 62 for humping coal.
Sacked, he wept for shame. They found him cold
in Wilf's bed. Son and father dug a hole
under the stars in God's acre (to save
the sexton's fee) then turfed his secret grave.

'38. In an R.A.F. latrine
Wilf and his mate Dan Cohen came on thugs
Beating a squaddie – "Yid, we'll scrub you clean" –
and beat *them*. Fascism, Racism, those drugs
maddening Europe, he'd good cause to fight –
a common, winning, cause. Next, to delight

in Labour's Dance – and bow out in despair
when Victory's quickstep changed to slow, slow, slow,
the Rich Ugly Old Maid sighing her Air
of prudence as the bright hopes lost their glow.
And as skies gathered to an icy dread
men turned blue in the cold, though he went Red.

Red for shame come '68. "Tanks on streets
kill hopes like men" he mourned, whose hopes yet flared
to light a way to Somewhere he might greet
Glad Day, its News of Now no more deferred.
Wilfred, that plain, good man, whose each least act
tells us that decency survives intact

beyond the headlines and that to read our age
rightly we must turn to History's Page.

OUT OF THE DARK

for Anne Stevenson

The car jollied its way down midnight lanes
after our Bosworth gig. *"Sweet especial rural scene"*
I sang, tipsily. Next thing – WHooSH – the windscreen
filled with white, before the shape lifted, planed

over and vanished, leaving behind a glare
that shook us all. "Now what in hell would stare
like that?" *"From* hell more like. Think Richard's ghost
come to protest at how the die was cast."

"Barn owl!" The pianist knew. "There's three-star food
for raptors in these hedgerows. Fieldmouse, stoat,
weasel or rabbit – minced, they taste as good
as steak tartar tipped down a gourmet's throat"

"Tough on stoats!" "A stoat will gorge on rabbit!"
"Fang, fur and claw in one convulsion hurled."
" 'Quote, unquote.' That's another nasty habit"
someone laughed. So I didn't pronounce your words:

and not one of them gened to protest against the world.

DYSTOPIC

"all poems about cats are twee." Sean O'Brien

Once, over 19c. Birmingham, frogs
rained thick as locusts, but in Athens, 1984, it was dogs
pelting hugger-mugger down a storm-swilled street,
harried by cats and still more cats slapping my feet
whenever I made to cross to the other side.

Mud-slathered fur, gone limbs and burst-wide eyes –
the Great Beast's stigmata. It was as if skies,
swagged like masque curtains above the raked city,
were leaking a denouement, some writerly
end made flesh, or rather shard-white bone and crusted blood.

For all were dead, and from them I understood
that "raining cats and dogs" entailed a gutter
churning with quadrupeds utterly
lacking grace as torrents denied them resting space
or piled them among gapped refuse bags, tyres, soleless shoes,

condoms thick as congers, gross
hydrocephalitic oranges oozing pus,
felix and *canus* suppurant at ear, nose, anus,
as they slewed through Athens's cloacal streets, debris
not chic, not sweet, not quaint, and, Sean, not twee.

THE DEATH OF THE HAT

a footnote to Billy Collins

Keen to flourish its exclusivity
my London (suburban) grammar school ruled
IN PUBLIC CAPS AT ALL TIMES *MUST* BE WORN.

That was fine by Peter West, class rebel
and apt recruit to Soldier Schweik's Platoon.
"West, your cap is a *disgrace*."

"I quite agree, Sir, and bought only this week."
The peak, scoured of stuffing,
Stuck to Pete's forehead like a misplaced ear.

"How, then, do you account for its appearance?"
The school Head was a Masonic Tory.
"Bad work, Sir? Shopfloor malcontents, perhaps?"

About that time my father,
gifted with unlooked-for City work,
hurried indoors a round, posh-leather box,

which, undone, freed clouds of tissue paper
and so disclosed to our astonished gaze
a vast black cabochon. My mother

bit her lip, hard, as the bowler
wobbled on his usually level head.
Next day the Drama Club gained one more prop.

Soon after, I read Edwin Muir on how
no Orknedian, however "rich, noble or powerful",
was ever called "Sir", and, as a matter of course,

"Scottish crofters refused to uncover their heads
before royalty." One day, because he failed
in Glasgow's cold to doff his workman's cap

while a superior person passed, young Muir's
ear got richly wacked. Taught his lesson,
from that day on Muir always went bareheaded.

TOWARDS THE VIA REPUBLICA

i) *School Assembly, February, 1952*

That swivel stare – a Lesser God
looking to finger some poor sod,
our crop-haired, sadist-suited Head,
Weeps as be blurts "the King is .... **Dead**",
and six who grin their disbelief
are caned into a state of grief.

ii) *Sunday Evensong, May, 1953*

The vicar, bowed in closing prayer,
haruspicates confidingly
"Her Coronation Day will be,
as God has surely planned it, fair."
The pews exhale a damp "amen."

Years on I hear that voice again
dress up its unctuous certainty
in pin-stripe vowels (ah, Dimbleby),
its unopposable *savoir-faire*
drowned in the blest, unceasing rain.

iii) *A Scottish Holiday, July, 1954*

At 6 sharp by the Odeon clock
John Wayne can sheathe his gun at last.
The music's cut, the curtains close
— then part again on a dull shock
of drums and brass, their roll and blast,
as, side-saddle, the queen, her pose
held twice nightly on every screen
comes unvariably into view
while loyal subjects rise and sing

"God Save …."
　　　　　　　But here I turn and see
The only one to rise is me!
"Sit doon", and then "ye're no *our* queen,
we canna stand the sight of you"
the rest shout. Sat at ease, they fling
butt ends, crisp packets, paper darts,
while harmonising chthonic farts
until the music fades and dies,
and only then they choose to rise.

Turning my back on her stiff gaze
I exit to a hirpling throng
of folk about their daily ways
and, wondering where I belong,
but pleased that I should get so far,
find myself in a public bar.

RANDYLOINS AND MURDOCH

(New Readers Begin Here)

Belinda lies abandoned on Mark's bed,
who's Petra's man, though Petra wants Belinda,
and, while sponging a fevered, puckered brow,
confesses to Jessica she would never hinder

her setting her cap at Saul, Belinda's son
by Marcus, who was Petra's first true beau,
Mark I for short, while Bee calls Mark, Mark 4,
and Mark calls Saul, who calls *him* quite *de trop*,

Jessica's Joint of Jism, and Petra weeps
with laughter at Mark's wicked turn of phrase,
while hoping it's not true Belinda's Golf
was seen near Godstow, windows all a haze,

and Jessica's Volvo parked nearby, though Saul
seems certain of it, for he'd trailed them there,
worn cords and brogues muddied from rutted paths
he'd biked in pale pursuit. Now, in despair

he mumbles over claret his belief
he can't be good in bed, while *she* thinks, should
she tell him it's not if you're good in bed
that counts, but if in bed you can be good?

THE BIOGRAPHER'S ART

He met her quite by chance upon the stairs.
He had been waiting for his chance.
Trembling, he begged her for the final waltz.
He led that girl a pretty dance.

"I love you" he dared to whisper then, lips dry.
We may surmise each trick he used.
She stopped his mouth. What more was there to say?
Her simple trust would be abused.

Their early married life was all a glow.
At first he thought lust spelled content.
She sang about the house, he worked in joy.
A trained eye spots the coming tyrant.

Crossing a busy street he'd take her hand.
Signs of coercion now appear.
Her beauty took away his busy words.
Some nights he barely spoke to her.

Years lapsed, the fresh blaze sifted down to gray.
Boredom he renamed rectitude.
Still they were warmed by stir of memories.
Her lost hopes proved a pelican brood.

She was the first to die, children about her.
Did he attend her last, hurt breath?
Bereft of all but heartache, he soon followed.
An arid life, a chilling death.

RETURN TO MERRYMOUNT

The mountains are high, the emperor far away,
We're free at last to live here as we choose.
No-one can tell us when to work or play.

The clocks are stopped. Each day is Holiday;
the gnomon quarters hours for sex and booze.
(The mountains are high, the emperor far away.)

The factory's torched, the maypole's here to stay,
we woke this morning, didn't have the blues:
no-one to tell us when to work or play.

No Plod to pry, no Suit to sigh or say
"But what of Soul?" "Verboten" or "J'accuse."
The mountains are high, the emperor far away.

Wasted – Tom, Dick, and Harry, each wide day,
Blitzed – Jack and Jill, on substance and self-abuse,
No-one can tell *them* when to work or play.

"This is the life!" we sing, or dancing, sway
to our new anthem "What's there left to lose,
The mountains are high, the emperor far away."

Who would confess that months of Come-What-May
begin to pall? We shuffle in our shoes.
The Mountains are high, the emperor far away.
Can *no-one* tell us when to work or play?.

THORSDAY

You sank your hammer deep in the giant's head
when you were after grub for friends. Unmoved,
"it felt like rain or birdshit", he declared

but later showed you mountains you had moved.
By then you'd failed to drink the sea, had found
lifting the earth too hard, and Old Age proved

so strong she bent you, struggling, to the ground.
These stories all agree you're dumb as an ox
poor Thor, a god of goodwill but unsound

wit, "a bohunk" in Odin's sneer. Mere rock
for brains, you sad, mad sod, to think you'd snare
the world's serpent with bull's head bait and hook!

Who says gods are not mocked? Yet still you dare
stacked odds to challenge berserks, garner more
of meat and drink your mates – some hope! – can share,

then scheme to break the troll's steel grip, make war
on the snake of Sturm and Kreig .... So, though it's true
such hopes at best are Winters' Tales, yet, Thor,

if I believed in gods I'd worship you.

YOURS SINCERELY

Dear Mr Lucus, I am instructed to thank you
for your visit to our literary group last week.
We were sorry to give you such short notice
but the gentleman we *wanted* to hear speak

died a few days earlier and left us in a pickle.
We could think of no substitute who would do,
had indeed quite scraped the bottom of the barrel.
Then someone suggested you.

This may explain why so few attended,
although it is true that on fine evenings
most people prefer to enjoy themselves,
and, as I always say, there is no reasoning

with those who will only stir for well-known names.
However, all four of us present
found much to think about over tea and cakes
(baked by Miss Tuck, our president –

who, I assure you, always listens with her eyes shut).
In closing, may I sincerely apologise
for putting you on board the 37 bus
which, as you no doubt came to realise,

unlike the 73 goes nowhere near the station.
Nevertheless I hope you were able to catch the last train
and that, should we in future ever need a last-minute stop gap,
we might perhaps call on your services again.

THORN'S WORK-OUT WEEK

Monday I've lined up Major Odes by Shelley,
Tuesday it's chill-out time in front of telly:
Wednesday's for Master Class down *Mister Man*
(Sun-dried *krill en-daube* or seared in the pan);

Thursday's pumping iron, flex the old pecs,
And Friday's set aside for Tantric Sex.
Come Saturday I'm with the Man U Lads
Then back to chapter 5 of *New Age Dads*.

Sunday we're at BAR NONE to neck a bottle
With doomy talk of pets – my axolotl
Will have to go, I think, it's so last year,
And Jade's macaw snuffed it with mossy ear.

Life's not all laughs! Jace asks if SARS can spread
From playing Chinese whispers.
                              Back in bed
With Tracey – she's still new – I play it cool.
Teacher needs shut eye to be fresh for school.

AN IMPROMPTU FIT OF RHYME ABOUT RHYME

for Richard Kell

Richard, I guess that we'll agree
which forms and measures guarantee
art's in good shape; for poetry
    we kiss the rod
of rhyme and metre, whereas free
    verse is a god

to whom we rarely bow the knee,
its service perfect anarchy
often, its Creed of "Let it be
    whatsoever"
the shapeless mud-pie recipe
    of kids playing clever,

for whom this feigning verse of Burns
is what the truest poet spurns:
"it cramps the mind, its rhyming turns
    like a stone wheel
that once ground corn in antique querns
    to powdered meal."

Rubbish! The dancing lore of rhyme
can pirouette in a sublime
entrechat or in good time
    turn sad or funny.
Allegro, Lento: discord, chime,
    dark or sunny.

And as for metres; what a choice!
What skraking bard would not rejoice
that English verse allows each voice
    to flex at will
its sound, the sweet especial noise
    that fits each bill.

For "will" read "skill". Without technique
truths that a writer sweats to seek
will be forgotten in a week,
      junked in the bin
where trash sincerities rot and reek.
      And you can't win

from Time Time's killing ways with stuff
that wasn't built to last; the rough
spur-of-the Moment job may bluff
      a first time buyer;
but give it time and the seeming-good-enough
      sinks in the mire.

What looked the smart buy of the week,
tres vie-en-mode, tres fort, tres chic,
will be abandoned, up the creek
      with other wrecks,
the unmapped graveyard for each clique
      gone down to dreck.

Thus Schoenberg's *mot* about C Major
gets my vote; and though I'll wager
that metronome called George L. Trager
      must loath the thought
that poetry even of sager
      kind is a sport,

it is, in Frost's sense. Drop the net
and the game's pointless. Point and set
and match will show us who's the bett-
      er player.
Who says Love-All is Art's Best Bet
      is art's betrayer.

Poetry's not just skill, of course:
that's bit and bridle without the horse,
Roy Campbell's point, who though a coarse
   and rough-shot wit,
knew just how lawless is the horse
   without the bit.

"I take my orders from the Muse" –
the claim of every fraud who views
the *tabla rasa* as good news
   for his blank vanity:
"We poets in our youth must choose
   to court insanity,

a garret life, bare boards, black bread,
the likelihood we'll soon be dead,
and nobody to share our bed."
   That brings them quick –
from Colour Supplements a head-
   strong swarm of thick

trend spotters with no need of art:
"Just sock it to us from the heart!
we'll see to it you top the chart
   Within a week"
And then? It's all Exchange and Mart
   and some new freak.

Fraud will batten on Fraud, and must
to live. But art is Derris Dust
to *aphis fabae.* "It's – well – just
   not where I'm at,
not *relevant*, a tad pie-crust,
   frankly old hat –

So *not* today." And they take flight –
a short day's journey into night
and art is spared their sticky blight.
        Six cheers for art
that scatters bugs in cloudy fright,
        and for my part

I'm pleased they fly before the fear
of metre, stanza, rhyme, the sheer
or curving rhythms that appear
        as jets of light,
that stream now snagged, now running clear,
        and all to delight

the ear. "And if your ear be true,
list mortals." Milton speaks for you
and everyone who'd wish to sue
        for the grace art gives
and blessedly receives, since through
        Art, art lives.

A MNEMONIC ALPHABET

for Bill Overton

A is for Amphimacer, chain and ball,
B is for Breve, barely heard at all;
C is for Choriamb, charmed to appear,
D is for Dimiter, it drums, is drear.
E is for Eclogue, a rustic effusion,
F is for Fancy or first prolusion.
G is for Gnomic, a guarding of words,
H is for Half-Rhyme, the hoarding of bards.
I is for Iamb, it must be so,
J is for Jongleur, the Geste of Bordeaux;
K is for Kenning, brought over the kite-pass,
L is for Lyric, sung to the looking-glass.
M is for Monometer, meanwhile
N is for Numbers and Nonce words like *skile*.
O is for Ode, Horatian or
P for Pindaric, its pristine ancestor.
Q is for Quantity, quite the long and short of it,
R is for Rhyme, where song really ought to fit.
S is for Spondee, spread wide, trod slow,
T is Tribach goes tiptoe:
U is for Ululate, grief upon air,
V is for Vocable, how it's voiced there;
W's the Wiles poets learn when they're older,
X is for Xeric, a cross they must shoulder;
Y is for Yawp, your poet as Yahoo,
Z is for Zebu: Laureates at the Zoo.

A PARTIAL HISTORY OF BRITISH JAZZ CLARINETTISTS

for John Mole

1

Start in that low, dishonest age
With jazz an *ersatz* suede-shoe rage.
The best it got was Harry Roy
Snowline high on *Chinaboy*,
Limehouse Blues, Chinatown,
Georgia and *Sweet Georgia Brown.*
Standards packaged for nightly use
By all who shook their morals loose
At svelte hotels, on Night-Club floors,
Those carious, titled, tight-faced boors,
Ideologues of etiquette
(Black ties for the Clivedon set),
Suits at all times, no booze on stand,
Jazz and Decorum hand-in-hand!
While Roy waxed hot on *Bugle Call*
Blue Blood coursed at the Jazz Band Ball.

2

War started and the music stopped.
Not quite three when bombs first dropped
And Café Society went bust,
Bowley and Snake-Hips blown to dust,
I heard the Siren voice of fear
Turn comatose at each All-Clear.

3

Years on I woke to radio news
Of Rags and Two-Steps, Stomps and Blues,
Each spoonful in a half-hour ration
Gulped down like malt: a strong, rich passion.
Sid Phillips had Geraldo licked,
Played by the Book, was tempo-strict,
But still he made me shift my feet
Onto the hot side of the street.
"Too commercial" snarled the purist.
Not for me! A wave-band tourist
I spun past worlds of Cotton Floss,
Hall, Payne and, worse, Edmundo Ross.
Though Sid might ride on leaden wings
He outsoared Mantovani's Strings,
And on his bumpy razz-ma-tazz
I lifted off to Planet Jazz.

4

Fast-forward now to '55.
Street Jazz, Pub Jazz: Jazz is Live!
Bands everywhere – what's in a name?
Apex, Strutters – all the same.
Each tyro clarinettist quotes
From Dodds' and Picou's quire of notes,
Then limps behind that wavering, sweet
Line drawn down Burgúndy Street
Leading adepts to London Town.
Wheeler, Semple, Sunshine, Brown,
Turner, Fawkes and Sammy R.
Take me where the good times are:
Humph's, Wood Green, the Winning Post,
The Club where Ken played Guru-Host,

And Eel-Pie Island most of all;
The bridge to Preservation Hall
It seemed we crossed as magical
Sounds washed down the summer Thames –
The Brown band in a Land of Dreams
That faded on the horn's last blues,
Though back it comes each time I choose
Blues McJazz to raise delight
And bring Hot Times to Town Tonight –
Tonight, Tomorrow and Every Night.

III

LAMENT FOR A DEAD SON

From the Old Norse of Egils Saga

My tongue, leaden with grief, lies
Listless, will not stir to song.
No poem moves in my mind,
My heart is heavy with tears.

So many tears! Such sadness!
All my thoughts are dark with death.
How can I breed song from such
Blackness? How quicken the breath?

Heart-soaking tears, like wild rain
Drenching the land. And the lash
Of wind on water! On Nain's
Rocks the sea splinters and howls.

My lineage ends, like storm-
Felled maples of the forest.
I have buried the bodies
Of too many of my kin.

I search for speech, for telling
Praise for my long-dead parents:
Words should bud in my mind now,
Blossom and blaze in green song.

The battering wave that broke
My father's line broke my life.
It smashed through as the wild sea
Breaches the widest sea wall.

Ran, you've dealt roughly with me.
My dearest friends are all dead,
And now you have slit the strand
Asgerd and I wove with love.

If a sword could heal this hurt
Aegir would brew no more beer.
I'd fling myself on that fierce
Wave-raiser and his mate, Ran.

But it seems I have no strength
To quell my dear son's killer.
In the minds of men I move
A mere lonely, thwarted man.

The sea has stripped me of much.
Bad and bitter work, to count
Dead kin, since Bodvar stepped out
Of life and lit on new paths.

No stuff of evil there. Son,
You would have grown to goodness,
But Odin snapped you before
Your sapling strength was full-branched.

Though others might disdain me
To him my words mattered most.
At home my word was his law,
His support gave me new strength.

And now I ponder the pain
A brother's death has brought me.
When the storms of battle swell,
I think of him and ask this:

Who now will stand by my side?
Who else will dare war's dangers?
For without my friends I need
Planned flight when I fight hard men.

A hard task, to find much trust
In any man now, anywhere.
Brother betrays brother, buys
Rings with his warm, bartered corpse.

Not thoughts of vengeance, but thoughts
Of gold goad men on these days.
Offer a man the money
And he'll lie, steal, slander, kill.

But nothing can now repay
Me for Bodvar's brutal death.
I can't sire another son
To stand for the son who's drowned.

And though men try to ease my
Pain I prefer solitude.
Dear son, with Odin now, son
Of Asgerd, you're with your kin.

But the cold and constant Sea-
God has left me lonely, wrecked,
And I cannot raise my head
Such weariness drags it down.

When fever killed my first son
Bodvar took all my best love.
I watched him grow strong and straight
And knew he was free of faults.

Such memories rise in my mind!
And then I think of Odin:
He tore this branch from my tree
And carried it clear away

To the high hall of the gods.
Odin has been good to me,
Yet I trusted him too much
And more than was good for me,

For he did allow that death.
Still, I sacrifice to him
— Not eagerly, but because
He gave my two great gifts

And they salve my heaviest hurts.
I owe my art to Odin,
So, too, my flaring temper,
Which make sure foes of all frauds.

And though all things go hard now
And Hel stands on the headland,
I wait her coming calmly,
Heart caulked, fit for my voyage.

Ran = "Ravisher": Wife of the Sea-God, Aegir, she owned a vast net in
which she tried to capture and draw to her any man who ventured onto the sea.
Asgerd = Egil's wife.
Hel = Goddess whose domain was the underworld.

DEATHFEAST

Adapted from the Greek of Takis Sinopoulos

Alone and writing, tears scalding me, what
were these voices, faces ....

so many years and
through the window came

resined light, benches and tables
set round and now

in they trooped: Porporas,
Kondaxis, Markos, Yerasimos,
Dismounting from a black mist of horses,
and as day slanted towards evening Bilias came,
Gournas, too, and Fakalos, swarthy in the half-light,
carrying mandolins, gypsy guitars, a flute,
music to lift the heart, and with them came
scent of wood and rain; then
when they'd lit a fire, a blaze to warm themselves,
and only then, I called a welcome to them.

My voice brought others: Sarris, Tsakonas,
Farnakis and Toregas and ...

Sour-faced, scarred by smallpox, in the prison camp at Akova
he dug the earth with his fingernails till they bled, and he
told me of rape, torture, his voice so dark it frightened me. I
ran off, slithering downhill

We went downhill, ashes everywhere scorched earth, twisted
iron, a black X painted on doors so you knew death had come
this way, days and nights our machine guns reaping and har-
vesting

you heard **Ah** *and nothing more*

65

Then others straggled in. Tsannis, Paparizos, Eleminoglou, and
behind,
Flaskis, Lazarides, Konstantopoulos – which churches mourned
for them,
who buried them, in what earth ….

Then I got him out from the ditch where he'd fallen, I held
him and he died in my arms, and a month after, in the deep
garden at midday, I told his wife of his death, her grass-sweet
scent, her full dark body whimpering against me, and at night
the woods glimmered, tree roots also

and after all these years her voice still comes to me

Moonlight froze, the days closed up, winter became a tower
of stone,
sunless, unyielding, I heard

a knock, another knock, as day broke they broke down the
doors and
dragged us out, breathless. 'Wait here, you,' and so little
light breaking.

Old men came, children too.
In such rags, how did they survive?
The old men's groans taller than their bodies,
and the children,
clasping a hatchet, a knife, an axe, in their eyes
contempt and menace, and not a word from them.

Ditches, rubbish tips, black-robed mothers wailing, whom
did you kill, whom did you kill

how many did we kill.

So much blood, Louka's severed hands, and other hands
chopped off, we'd
find them in the ravine months later as we left,

always on the run, here by day, at night somewhere else,

murderers, informers, thieves, adulterers, policemen,
house-owners,
shopkeepers

and many others riding the backs of those times, among them
desperate girls who took to the streets, hungry, feverish,
who did it up
against a wall, an evil wind blowing.

And now there came

Litsa and Fani, apple-ripe, Dona and Nana, slender as wheat,
Eleni,
budding like a laurel tree,

vine-shoots, myrtles,
small lost rivers

And one morning

that morning when I woke the tree was all green, I loved it so
that it reached up to the sky

and birds flocked to it, glittering like joy in the new sun, they
filled the place with movement, colour, sound, perlicams and
others just as strange, wagtrailers, crumplecocks, offlanders,
skylurkers and

gifts of God, images of delight endlessly wheeling through
blue air. Among them came

Makris, Kallinikos, clubfoot Yannis.

We sat down on a tump, Rouskas took out his pocket-knife,
slashed at the
new-grown grass

the field a haze, and spring coming, you could hear it.
A door whose wood smelled of sky.

And then the door slammed to.
Days of '44
then days of '48.
And from the Peloponnesos to Larissa
Down as far as Kastoria
a black infection covered the map,
Greece gasping for breath, —
at Easter in desolate Kozani we held a count,
how many had stayed on high land, who'd journeyed on
down the dark river ....

Prosoras came in now, shouldering his patched-up rifle,
Bakrisioris, Alafouzos, Zervos,

Tzeptetis, Zafoglou, Markoutsas,
threw themselves down on a bench,
Constantinos nursing his wounded foot.
Look I shouted
and they looked.

Light poured in from the fruit-bearing sun
in memory of the lost ones. So many years have passed
I told them, our hair's turned grey.

Little by little the voices died,
each face turned from me, one by one they left.
They took to the valley, they dwindled into air.

For the last time I gazed after them, called to them.
The fire wasted to ash and through the window I saw

how with just one star the night turns navigable

how in an empty church the nameless dead
are lain among heaped flowers, are anointed.

My grateful thanks to Dr Manos Georginis without whose expert guidance this version
of Sinopoulos's poem would have been impossible.